RED TARA COMMENTARY

Red Tara Commentary

INSTRUCTIONS FOR THE
CONCISE PRACTICE KNOWN AS
RED TARA: AN OPEN DOOR
TO BLISS AND ULTIMATE AWARENESS

Compiled from the teachings of
His Eminence Chagdud Tulku Rinpoche by

Chagdud Khadro

PADMA PUBLISHING
1999

Published by
Padma Publishing
P.O. Box 279
Junction City, CA 96048-0279

© Padma Publishing 1986
Second edition 1994

Printed in the United States of America
Third Printing, 2003

ISBN 1-881847-04-7

Contents

CONTENTS

Preface

IN THIS REVISED and reformatted edition
of the *Red Tara Commentary*, various errors
have been corrected and stylistic changes
made. This edition also includes instructions
for sections not in the original practice text:
the mandala offering, the feast offering and
the meditation for the dead.

Once again I thank all those who have
helped produce this book and Chagdud
Tulku Rinpoche, who has offered me the
great privilege of presenting his teachings.
May the powerful flow of his intention and
his example inspire all who read this book
and meditate on Red Tara. May all beings
benefit.

Jane Tromge
[Chagdud Khadro]
Rigdzin Ling, California
Fall 1993

Preface to the First Edition

THESE WRITTEN INSTRUCTIONS for the concise Red Tara practice come from my wish that others might gain as much benefit as I have from Tara meditation. My life has been very fortunate, but still, as with all beings caught in samsaric confusion, there have been times of emotional and mental turmoil, times of illness.

In those times, by the compassion of my heart's lama, Chagdud Tulku Rinpoche, I have had a reliable method to work through obstacles, to find deep levels of comfort not dependent on outer circumstances and to penetrate, if only momentarily, the obscuring cover of my mind's delusion. This method is Red Tara practice, and since having been given this wish-fulfilling gem, my life has gained rich meaning and focus.

As I wish blessing and full accomplishment of Tara practice for myself, I also wish this for all others. I hope that these instructions help and clarify your practice. I apologize in advance for any mistakes in this first edition. The instructions are meant to be used in conjunction with the short Tara practice text published by Padma Publishing. Also, they are not meant to stand on their own, but to supplement oral transmission by a qualified teacher.

Even a small project such as this book has required enormous help from many of my vajra brothers and sisters, particularly Tsering Everest, without whose insightful and intelligent translation of the teachings these instructions could not have been written.

Beyond simple gratitude, I bow in reverence before my precious teacher, Chagdud Rinpoche, whose faith in Westerners' ability to comprehend the sacred Buddhadharma is unsurpassed and who displays Tara's blessings as wisdom nectar, rainbow light and fireworks.

Jane Tromge
Cottage Grove, Oregon
April 1986

Introduction

The Story of Tara

Countless aeons ago, in a time beyond the beginning of our time, a buddha appeared in a worldly realm called "Various Lights." A princess in that realm, named Moon of Wisdom (Tib. Yeshe Dawa), developed great faith in and devotion toward the buddha. She paid homage with body, speech and mind, making immeasurable offerings to him and his retinue. When, by virtue of her vast accumulations of merit and pristine awareness, the thought of supreme enlightenment awakened in her, the monks of the realm advised her to pray for rebirth in a male body, for they thought that such a body would be a superior vehicle for enlightenment.

Because Yeshe Dawa had realized the empty nature of all phenomena, she recognized that there was no inherent reality in either the male body or the female body.

Confronted by the relative reality of ignorant insistence on such differentiations, however, she made the commitment always to take re-birth in female form.

Eventually she attained a profound medi-tative state from which she was able to place innumerable beings in realms beyond suffer-ing. In our own world system she manifested as Tara through the compassion of Avaloki-teshvara (Tib. Chenrezi), and here she made the particular vow to liberate beings from eight great fears that are the projections of negativities within the mind. These are fear of elephants as the projection of ignorance, of fire as the projection of anger, of lions as pride, of robbers as false views, of floods as avarice, of snakes as jealousy, of handcuffs (imprisonment) as miserliness and of demons as doubt. This traditional delineation of fears encompasses all the fears and phobias that arise from our habits of attachment and aver-sion. Ultimately Tara offers liberation from any fear of samsaric suffering. For this reason she is called the Swift Savioress.

History of the Lineage of Red Tara

Tara is the female buddha. Although all feminine deities are aspects of and inseparable from her, we pay particular homage to twenty-one Taras who emanate as goddesses of the padma, vajra, ratna and karma families. The methods we use to attain the enlightened qualities of Tara have been passed down through many perfect lineages of highly realized Tibetan Buddhist practitioners.

The lineage of this Red Tara meditation practiced under the guidance of Chagdud Tulku Rinpoche began in an exalted way in the intentional mind of Amitabha Buddha. From Amitabha it passed to Avalokiteshvara and then to an emanation of Tara herself. From Tara it went to the renowned Indian Buddhist master Nagarjuna and then to Padmasambhava, the great Buddhist teacher who brought vajrayana Buddhism to Tibet in the ninth century. Padmasambhava gave this teaching to the son of the Tibetan king Trisong Detzen. He also gave it to his wisdom consort, Yeshe Tsogyal, and asked that she hide it as a treasure to be discovered at a later time, when it would produce the most benefit.

Thus, the treasure of the Red Tara cycle was discovered and codified more than a thousand years after Padmasambhava, by Apong Terton, a great Nyingmapa lama who lived in this century. Its formal title is *The Condensed Essence of the Treasure of Supreme Enlightened Mind: The Mandala Ritual of the Noble Red Tara Called the Wish-Fulfilling Essence.*

At the end of his life, Apong Terton summoned a monk whom he had initiated into Red Tara and told him, "I am dying—I ask that you do something for me. When I am seventeen years old in my next incarnation, come to me and give me the initiation and oral transmissions of the complete Red Tara treasure."

After Apong Terton died, the Chinese consolidated their conquest of Tibet, and the monk, like so many others, was forced to flee. He became a refugee in the small country of Bhutan. Apong Terton reincarnated as His Holiness Sakya Trizin, head of the Sakyapa tradition of Tibetan Buddhism. When Sakya Trizin was seventeen years old, the monk tried to go to him at a place near Dehra Dun in northern India, but he could not get a passport. It was not until several years later that he, appearing rather ragged in the richly ornamented meditation hall of Sakya Trizin's monastery, was able to meet his former teacher.

A few moments after the monk spoke to Sakya Trizin, the assembly of monks in the shrine room was surprised to be dismissed and to learn that His Holiness would take initiation from the outwardly undistinguished visitor. The monk then gave the Red Tara initiation to Sakya Trizin and Sakya Trizin's remarkable sister, Jetsunma.

On his way to meet Sakya Trizin, the monk encountered Chagdud Rinpoche, who was in Tso Pema, a sacred site in the Himalayas of northern India where Padmasambhava had meditated with Mandarava, one of his great wisdom consorts. Rinpoche had always had a connection to Tara practice—his mother, a famous lama, was in fact an emanation of Tara. He had accomplished extensive Tara practice in retreat, but despite his affinity for red deities of the padma family, he had never received a Red Tara practice. In

Tso Pema he had many auspicious dreams indicating that soon his ability to benefit others would greatly increase.

Upon meeting him, the monk suggested to Rinpoche that if he were given the Red Tara empowerment, great benefit would ensue. Rinpoche agreed and after receiving the initiation from the monk made an extended Red Tara retreat, during which he experienced many signs of accomplishment.

Although Rinpoche became renowned for his miraculous activities as a Tara practitioner, he did not teach the practice widely until he came to the United States fifteen years later. In 1980 he began teaching Red Tara to some students in Oregon, guiding their development in the steps of visualization and offerings.

THE RED TARA TREASURE is an extensive cycle that includes preliminary practices, dream yoga, healing practices, yoga of the subtle channels and energies (Tib. *tza lung*) and extensive teachings on the nature of mind. The main practice has been translated and is performed regularly at Chagdud

Gonpa centers. The steps of the Red Tara practice are interspersed with prayers of homage to the twenty-one Taras written by another great Nyingmapa lama, a contemporary of Apong Terton, Khenpo Ngaga.

Chagdud Rinpoche has also distilled the essence of the practice in a more accessible, concise English version. This shorter text contains two levels of practice: the first is a visualization of Tara in the space in front of oneself that does not require initiation; the second involves visualization of oneself as Tara and does require initiation. Through initiation, the blessings of the lineage are formally transmitted and one's mind is ripened in order to realize the profundity of the practice.

Chagdud Rinpoche uses the short English text as the framework for Tara dream yoga and healing practices. Like all Tibetan liturgies (Skt. *sadhana*), the text is divided into three sections—the preliminary prayers, the main practice and the concluding prayers. The explanation of the English practice offered in the present book is similarly divided and closes with some advice on how to use Tara meditation in daily practice.

Preliminary Prayers

Seven-Line Prayer

The sadhana begins, as do all sadhanas in the Nyingmapa tradition of Tibetan Buddhism, with the Seven-Line Prayer to Guru Rinpoche (Padmasambhava). The prayer invokes his blessings as the unsurpassed Buddhist master who brought vajrayana to Tibet and who is a lineage source of this Red Tara practice.

The Tibetan term for vajrayana is *sang ngak,* "secret, very swift path." The direct methods of vajrayana are used to free the mind from the five mental poisons—anger, grasping, ignorance, jealousy and pride. These poisons obscure recognition of one's skylike buddha nature, the uncontrived awareness that is intrinsic to all beings. To glimpse this intrinsic awareness, one must rely on a lama whose knowledge transcends

mere intellectual understanding, who has stabilized his or her recognition of mind's nature
through meditative realization. Invocation
and prayer to Guru Rinpoche render the practitioner receptive to the blessings of such lineage lamas, inseparable from Guru Rinpoche.

This Red Tara practice, as a complete
vajrayana sadhana, holds the full potential to
remove mind's obscuring cover and reveal its
natural qualities of compassion and pristine
awareness. The realized lama holds the key to
the practice. The perfect qualities of the
lama's realization are acknowledged and
called forth in the Seven-Line Prayer to Guru
Rinpoche. While praying, one should visualize Guru Rinpoche, but it is even more important to have faith in the power of vajrayana
and in the lama as the embodiment of
vajrayana.

Invocation

The second preliminary step is the invocation of the noble Red Tara as the mother of
all the victorious ones. At this point the luminous form of Tara appears in the space in
front of oneself. Development of the visual-

ization will be outlined in the chapter on the main practice.

Here it is important to understand why Tara is called the mother of all the victorious ones. Was she simultaneously the princess who paid homage to a buddha and the mother of that buddha? The answer, at the level of absolute truth, is yes. Tara is the mother space of emptiness, the dharmakaya, the ground of all phenomena. As the dharmakaya mother, she is the source and the spontaneous display of clarity that is the sambhogakaya, and the compassionate emanation of emptiness and clarity inseparable that is the nirmanakaya. *Kaya*, the Sanskrit word for "body," refers to spheres of truth.

This invocation of Tara establishes at the outset that the practice is based on an exalted level of understanding. Tara meditation takes one beyond verbal descriptions of the three kayas toward nonconceptual recognition of their absolute inseparability.

Bodhichitta

The third preliminary step is the affirmation of bodhichitta intention to attain enlight-

enment and to work for the welfare of all beings until they too find ultimate liberation.
Usually refuge is recited before bodhichitta,
but here one first affirms one's compassion
and the altruistic intention to help all beings
find lasting happiness as the motivation for
taking refuge in the perfect qualities of Tara.

Buddhism is sometimes thought of as a
bleak spiritual path, with its emphasis on the
suffering of samsara. Yet clearly acknowledging suffering is the first step in finding a way
out and a tonic for all our false hopes, our
tendencies to rely on ephemeral pleasures
that leave an aftermath of disappointment.

We need only watch the television news to
be confronted by immense suffering—need
only reflect on the painful events in the lives of
those around us or explore the continual un-
dertow of our own problems to confirm that
sorrow and misery pervade existence. Such
recognition can overwhelm and weary us. We
wonder how it came about, without really ex-
pecting an answer. Buddhist teachings, however, are clear on this point. Suffering, in all
its countless manifestations, has a single
source, the delusion of the dualistic mind.

To understand this confusion at its source, imagine a state in which phenomena arise and subside naturally with no differentiation of self and other. This undifferentiated awareness suddenly stirs into a slight apprehension of something other, then contracts around a subtle sense of self. Differentiation of color and shape comes into play, followed by the afflictive emotions of attraction and aversion, grasping and avoidance, hope and fear.

Next, these dualistic tendencies bring about fictitious formations, both elemental and mental, of self and grosser projections of other. As the whole mind–body makeup becomes increasingly dense, beings take rebirth after rebirth in bodies and realms that correspond to the tendencies that develop in their mindstreams. They are subject to the karmic outcomes created by these tendencies, but, lost in the patterns of dualistic confusion, they are unable to trace karmic events back to their source in the mind. In their ignorance, they attribute tragedies to blows of fate, unexpected triumphs to luck. They do not see that all aspects of their situation, including the bodies they inhabit, have been self-created over countless lifetimes.

The dualistic mind, the mind that grasps at self and gives self-interest priority over the interests of others, arises as the five poisons, which in turn lead to six types of rebirth: ignorance leading to rebirth as an animal, greed to rebirth as a hungry spirit, anger to rebirth as a hell being, jealousy combined with some virtue to rebirth as a jealous god (also known as a demigod), pride combined with virtue to rebirth as a long-lived god (deva) and great virtue combined with a mixture of all five poisons to rebirth as a human.

Once we know that such poisons are the inevitable cause of pain, of all the problems of existence, we feel deep compassion and a heartfelt commitment to find a way out for all who "are lost in the ocean of samsaric suffering." Liberation from the confusion and suffering of samsara—both our own liberation and that of others—comes about when obscuring dualistic patterns are cleared away, mind's absolute nature is recognized and this recognition is stabilized as an omniscient state beyond any concept of self and other—that is, buddhahood.

No one, not a terrorist, or a child, or ourselves in our darkest moments of confusion, or the gods and demons of unseen realms, or a dull old family dog—not the tiniest one-celled animal or the grandest creature in the universe—is ever apart from an innate potential for buddhahood. For this reason, there is the exalted hope that in attaining buddhahood we may bring temporary and ultimate happiness to ourselves and all other beings.

Those who seek buddhahood for the welfare of all beings are bodhisattvas, awakened ones who dispel delusion in each moment by awareness and thus benefit others. The Tibetan phrase for "bodhisattva" is *jang chub sem pa*. *Jang* means that self-grasping and self-importance decrease until all obstacles to enlightenment are gone. *Chub* indicates that the qualities of a good heart and altruistic intention increase until absolute compassion and pristine awareness (Skt. *jnana;* Tib. *ye she*) are realized. *Sem* means mind and *pa* comes from *pa wo* or *pa mo,* "hero" or "heroine," respectively. Thus, "bodhisattva" can be translated as "one of heroic mind who follows the path of purification and altruistic intention to benefit others."

In Tibetan one of the terms for buddha nature is *jang chub nying po,* meaning "essence of enlightenment." Thus, a buddha is one who follows the bodhisattva path to the very heart of enlightenment. In a buddha's mind there is complete illumination without a trace of delusion. A buddha's enlightened mind is omniscient, simultaneously encompassing within its awareness the single, absolute, empty nature of phenomena and the multiplicity of their specific details and patterns of interrelatedness.

The term "buddha" refers not only to the historical Shakyamuni, whose example we revere, but to the countless beings who have reached buddhahood during the innumerable aeons of the infinite universe. It also refers to our own intrinsic nature, which is never lost but remains unrecognized because of the dense obscuration caused by our dualistic concepts. When we say, "I seek buddhahood," we commit ourselves to following the examples of the buddhas and bodhisattvas in revealing the buddha nature within ourselves and all beings.

WHERE DO WE BEGIN? How do we make the seeking of buddhahood a vital, ongoing process when we are so immersed in our confusion that buddhahood is a state beyond our comprehension? What are the first steps and methods of the path?

Behind the inspiration to follow the bodhisattva path are four qualities: equanimity, compassion, love and joy. Equanimity inspires us to hold all beings equally, without attachment for some, aversion for others. Compassion inspires us to alleviate the suffering of others; love to seek their happiness and the cause of happiness, which is virtue; joy to delight truly in whatever virtue and happiness others gain. As these four qualities are developed and increase into vast, nondual wisdom, they are known as the "four immeasurables."

To engage in the path of the bodhisattva, we undertake the six trainings ("Six Perfections" or "Six Paramitas") of generosity, moral discipline, patience, joyful perseverance, concentration and transcendent knowledge. These six trainings are like keys that open each moment into awareness, enabling us to actualize our equanimity, compassion, love and joy. For example, the compassionate wish to free others from suffering is acted upon as a generous willingness to meet their needs. Compassion is a clear, strong choice that we can sustain when we have the moral discipline to know what to accept and what to reject. Our compassionate intention prevails in adversity because we are patient and persevere. It is focused and one-pointed through concentration.

The sixth training, transcendent knowledge or wisdom (Skt. *prajna;* Tib. *she rab*), is nondual recognition of phenomena as having no inherent self-nature. Transcendent knowledge should be understood to be inseparable from the first five trainings and the four immeasurables. As we hear the teachings on these qualities and contemplate them in a conceptual way, we begin to experience them in meditation as nonconceptual, spontaneous expressions of wisdom. Ultimately, as we find liberation from the fictitious delineations of self, other and the interaction between them, barriers between the spontaneous display of these pure qualities and our manifestation of body, speech and mind fall away. This is the actualization of buddha nature; this is the process of becoming enlightened.

Refuge

We take refuge in Tara as a buddha, inseparable from the stainless illumination and omniscience of a buddha. This is the refuge of enlightened mind.

We also take refuge in Tara as the dharma, the sacred teachings of Buddha Shakyamuni—the texts, oral transmissions, sacred mantras and prayers. This is the refuge of enlightened speech.

Further, we take refuge in Tara as the sangha, those who follow the teachings of Buddha Shakyamuni. This is the refuge of enlightened body.

As the Buddha, dharma and sangha are the supreme Three Jewels, the lama, yidam and dakini are the Three Roots. The lama is a buddha and, by being present to guide us in this life, shows us greater and more direct kindness than even Buddha Shakyamuni. *La* means "high" and *ma* means "mother." The lama is the one who is more precious than life itself, whose compassion is greater than that of a mother for her only child. Like the Buddha, the lama is a perfect and complete source of refuge.

The yidam is the meditational deity with whom one has an abiding connection. The yidam, in every aspect of body, speech and mind, expresses the pure qualities of buddhahood. *Yid* means "mind" and *dam* comes from *dam tsik,* which means "spiritual commitment." By maintaining the commitments of deity practice, we develop the pure, perfect qualities of the yidam as our own natural expression and realize the nature of the deity as none other than our own intrinsic nature.

The yidam is like a fully opened flower. We have the seed of the same flower within us. By our faith and meditation, and by the blessings of the lamas who show us the seed and how to cultivate it, we make it flourish into the full flower of the yidam.

Dakini, a Sanskrit word, is *kha dro ma* in Tibetan. *Kha* means "sky," *dro* means "goer" and *ma* means "mother." The *kha dro ma* is the sky dancer, the incomprehensible feminine wisdom, that realizes completely the empty nature of phenomena and thus goes without obstruction through space as the agent of enlightened activities.

TAKING REFUGE IN TARA as the Three Jewels and Three Roots, we acknowledge her as inseparable from them and from the facets of enlightenment that they represent. Even as we recognize Tara as an object of refuge, we need to understand what this means to us as the ones taking refuge.

Alexander Berzin, a translator for His Holiness the Dalai Lama, commented on the connotation of the word "refuge" as a translation of the Tibetan term. He pointed out that "refuge" conveys a sense of isolation, of withdrawing into an ivory tower, whereas what it is meant to represent is an active process, a constant engaging of the dharma path. He himself uses an alternative translation, "wholehearted commitment."

Once we have made our commitment of faith in Tara, an extraordinary sense of blessing and protection envelops us. We experience a connection to the buddhas and bodhisattvas, to all the lineage lamas who have realized the practice before us and to Tara as the Swift Savioress whose vow is to protect all beings if they do nothing more than call her name.

Chagdud Rinpoche sometimes says that the blessings of the wisdom beings and our refuge commitment are like a hook and eye. The infinite compassion and love of the wisdom beings are always there for us, unwavering, absolute. It is the supreme intention of the buddhas that all beings find a way out of the ocean of samsara and attain a state of pristine awareness. Yet the hook of enlightened intention must connect with the eye of our own faith, and this is accomplished by taking refuge. The interdependence of our faith and the blessings of the wisdom beings creates a sense of refuge that is much greater than our commitment alone. It is like stepping through an open doorway and finding oneself in a realm of transformation where every phenomenon has spiritual meaning and can be used to attain ultimate freedom and happiness.

The basis of the refuge commitment is to refrain from harming. To hurt others, and particularly to kill them, is directly opposed to the enlightened intention that all beings be free of suffering and find happiness. Harming and killing contradict Tara's very name, which in Tibetan is Drolma, literally, "liberation [*drol*] mother [*ma*]"—the Mother of Liberation. Her vow and her example are to protect and save beings.

A contested issue in the United States centers on assisting the death of persons and animals in order to put them out of their misery. Chagdud Rinpoche was once asked what he thought "idiot compassion" meant. He replied that he couldn't think of any compassionate act to alleviate suffering that could be considered idiotic except mercy killing. This is because the rebirth and suffering that follow such a death may actually be much worse than the present condition.

He also said that one moment of suffering in the human realm purifies karma that would result in centuries of suffering in the hell realms, because humans can maintain awareness that transcends pain. Hell beings are lost in fathomless pain and have no comprehension of anything beyond their own suffering. They can only wait until the karma that caused their suffering is exhausted by an equal measure of torment, whereas humans can shortcut suffering by acknowledging its source in their karma as individuals and by developing empathy and compassion for the suffering of others.

True mercy, therefore, is using the power of our meditation, our prayers and our activities to turn the focus of suffering beings away from the grinding limitations of the habitual mind and toward the transcendent view of innate buddha nature. Ultimately, in a state of open, nondual awareness, one recognizes the emptiness of appearances and knows that even the most solid substances are impermanent, mutable and without inherent reality. Likewise, one recognizes that painful phenomena, even their most intense physical and emotional ramifications, are in essence empty. If one can experience pain and simultaneously sustain recognition of its illusory nature, one can free oneself from great mental suffering, which may decrease physical suffering as well.

Our ability to help others achieve such recognition corresponds to the understanding we have developed within ourselves. The practice of Red Tara is a supreme vehicle for arousing both intellectual understanding and meditative realization of nondual awareness. While the name of Tara is Drolma, the name of this particular emanation as Red Tara is Rigjed Lhamo, Goddess Who Brings Forth One's Own Natural Awareness. When the practice is fully accomplished, it is pure, nondual awareness itself that provides refuge. This is the complete fulfillment of our practice commitment and Rigjed Lhamo's great blessing to those who take refuge in her.

Main Practice

Visualization: Symbolic Aspects of Tara

We visualize the luminous form of the noble Tara in the space in front of us. She is the brilliant ruby red of the padma (lotus) family deities, red signifying desire in its pure, most exalted aspect, the desire that all beings find liberation. The padma family deities are associated with enlightened speech.

Tara wears a crown studded with the gems of the five buddha families, and she is adorned with the other jeweled ornaments and silken garments of the sambhogakaya deities. These ornaments are the crown, ear-rings, three lengths of necklaces, bracelets, armlets and anklets. The silken garments include a long stole, a brocade bolero, pendants hanging from the crown and a short skirt. Tara's sambhogakaya garb symbolizes her enjoyment of the full wealth of pure percep-tions. The ornaments and garments are worn perfectly, yet merely as adornments of her nonattachment.

She is radiant, smiling and very beautiful. Half of her hair is in a knot at the crown of her head, expressing the gathering of all perfect qualities into the *ushnisha*, the spherical protrusion that is one of the marks of enlightened body. Half of her hair flows down her back, expressing the boundless freedom of uncontrived, intrinsic awareness. Her three eyes symbolize her embodiment of the three kayas. She is the emptiness of the dharmakaya. Yet this emptiness is not voidness, because the dharmakaya holds the full potential of appearance. In nondual awareness, appearances are radiant, spontaneous, the display of clarity of the sambhogakaya. The sambhogakaya aspect of Tara is what we represent in art and what we visualize.

Perceived through the habitual mind, however, appearances are the denser emanations of the nirmanakaya. The nirmanakaya is what we ordinarily experience as the elements—earth, wind, water, fire, space—and their myriad form manifestations as people, mountains, oceans, automobiles, plants and

so forth. Yet Tara is not apart from the nirmanakaya. For the benefit of sentient beings,
she emanates as lamas and statues, as practitioners and friends, as helpers who turn up
suddenly in threatening situations. Ultimately, all that appears in the nirmanakaya is
recognized as her emanation and is experienced as absolutely inseparable from dharmakaya emptiness and sambhogakaya clarity.

Her right hand, in the gesture of supreme
generosity, holds a long-life vase. Supreme
generosity means the bestowal of the supreme
realization of enlightenment. However, it in
no way excludes ordinary generosity, protection from the eight great fears or the manifestation of whatever we need for temporary
happiness and well-being. In particular, the
long-life vase Tara holds indicates that she offers whatever is necessary to sustain long life.

One of the paradoxes of Buddhist practice
is that we achieve a certain detachment from
our bodies and lose some measure of our fear
of death. Yet at the same time, we come to
understand how precious our human bodies
are—how useful for spiritual development—
and we pray that death will not interrupt our

practice. We want to increase and stabilize our attainment and accomplish as much as we can as bodhisattvas working for the welfare of all beings. So we should not be reluctant to pray to Tara for the preservation of our lives or the lives of others. As we pray, we acknowledge that all beings try to protect their own lives and request that Tara bestow long life on all who would benefit from longevity. Sooner or later the forces of impermanence and death will intervene, and we should have faith that Tara is as generous in death as in life, that she can give complete liberation in the after-death transition.

Because generosity and bountifulness are so characteristic of Red Tara, we should remember in developing these qualities in ourselves that true generosity remains devoid of attachment. Everything is an offering used to create temporary and ultimate happiness. Even our food, as we partake of it, is increased through visualization and recitation and is offered as nourishment to the entire universe.

The lamas themselves are wonderful examples of generosity, offering whatever is needed to whoever comes to them. If people need tea, they are given tea; if they need training, they are given training. One time a student brought her broken mala (string of prayer beads) to Chagdud Rinpoche, and he began to restring it. A visitor commented that it was odd that the lama should do this tedious task for his student, and Rinpoche replied, "Why? It brings her happiness and creates virtue for me."

Again, in Nepal, where Rinpoche lived before coming to the United States, he was in the habit of giving food to anyone who was around at mealtimes. He did not have much money, and the student who cooked for him became concerned about making ends meet. The opportunity to discuss the matter privately came one day when Rinpoche went up to the roof of his residence and began to offer leftover tormas (ritual sculptures made of barley flour) to the birds.

As scores of raucous crows swooped down and attacked the pieces of torma, the student explained that there would soon be no money to feed anyone, not even Rinpoche himself, if he continued to offer sustenance to everyone who stopped in for a visit. Listening patiently, tossing tormas to the crows, Rinpoche simply said, "Give. Don't worry, just give."

Suddenly a crow overhead let his own little offering fall, plop!, on Rinpoche's shoulder. Rinpoche burst out laughing. "You see? I give him these tormas and he gives me this!" The student later saw that the crow's offering had perhaps been a good omen, because as the guests multiplied, so did the food, and so did wealth and well-being in general.

As our realization of Tara increases, generosity becomes easier, more spontaneous and more accurate in terms of others' needs. We recognize the essential emptiness of ourselves as the offerer, of those who receive our offering, and of the act of offering itself. When these three spheres (Tib. *khor sum*) are recognized as one, we attain complete generosity inseparable from transcendent knowledge of the empty nature of offering.

As Tara's right hand is in the mudra (or gesture) of supreme generosity, so the left is in the mudra of the Three Jewels. This means that Tara is the embodiment of the Three

Jewels and completely expresses the perfect qualities of Buddha, dharma and sangha.

In her left hand she holds the stem of a red utpala flower, which blossoms by her ear and contains in its center a fully drawn bow and arrow made of small lotus flowers. The bow symbolizes skillful means, the arrow pristine awareness.

She sits on a red lotus, which cups a sun disk. The lotus symbolizes faultlessness, the sun disk pristine awareness. A full rising moon behind her symbolizes skillful means. She sits in the posture of royal ease, her left foot tucked up, signifying that she is never apart from the bliss of nirvana; the right leg slightly extended shows that she manifests her perfection equally in samsara.

She is surrounded by a glorious rainbow-light aureole containing the radiant colors of the five aspects of pristine awareness—white, red, blue, green and yellow—which will be explained in the section on meditation and recitation.

WE VISUALIZE TARA as an effulgent light body, saturated with rich color, sparkling with brilliant jewels, surrounded by an orb of intense rainbow-light radiance. There is not a single particle of solidity in all this, yet we should develop a sense of Tara's presence as palpable as that of another person in the room with us.

At first this may prove difficult. Sometimes our minds are too distracted to visualize at all, or our sense of Tara's appearance is so dim that she seems faded, out of focus, with details missing. When this happens, we should concentrate on some aspect we hold firmly—her face or a hand gesture or an ornament whose significance intrigues us. Or we might focus on her presence within her powerful field of radiance and the emanation of purifying light and positive qualities.

The important point is to bring the mind back to a particular aspect of practice. We want to hold a clear visual image of Tara, so we study artistic representations or we visualize some part of her form until it is very clear in our mind's eye. We want to understand her qualities, so we attend teachings and contemplate Tara's symbolic aspects. During meditation, however, we seek to expand what we know conceptually into a state of nondual awareness. To do this we must make meditation very natural, not straining too hard toward perfect visualization, not trying to remember every detail. Instead, we simply remain within the flow of meditation, without straying too far into ordinary thoughts, sensory distractions and emotions. Ordinary mind-forms, particularly thoughts, will arise, but we simply let them dissolve into mind's natural spaciousness. And again and again, we turn to Tara.

Chagdud Rinpoche says that the mind-stream, continually redirected into meditation, flowing past mundane mind-forms, is like a river flowing over boulders—the water is purified each time it runs up against stone. One finally realizes that even stone, seemingly so impervious and solid, has the basic nature of emptiness.

However, when the flow of meditation becomes diverted and frustrated by the obstructions of the habitual mind, Rinpoche advises his students to return to the very source of spiritual attainment, which is the bodhichitta intention to benefit all beings. No obstacle in meditation has more power than the power of bodhichitta.

If we remember the profound suffering of others and reaffirm our intention to gain realization for their sake as well as our own, obstacles give way. Later we can look back and know that those obstacles were only transparent roadblocks on an illusory road within the infinite expanse of Tara's wisdom.

Meditation and Recitation

Invoking the noble Red Tara in the space in front of us, we recite the prayers of refuge and bodhichitta, and establish the visualization. As we begin reciting the Jetzun Prayer, we visualize as follows.

"A brilliant surge of rainbow light" beams from Tara's forehead, throat and heart, purifying all negative karma, "sickness, demonic afflictions and obstacles." All positive qualities "increase beyond measure."

As Tara's light radiates forth, blue light purifies the karma of anger, red light desire, white light ignorance, green light jealousy, yellow light pride.

We visualize this as really happening, envisioning that red light, for example, completely pervades samsara and empties every being in it of delusive desire, that the whole spectrum of lust, craving, obsession, desire and attachment—from the most murderous rapacity to the yogin's last trace of self-clinging—vanishes, dissolving into its own empty nature.

We check our minds for attachments and think about how we hold on to everything—people, pets, jobs, houses, clothes, ideas, emotions, situations—as real. We realize that although our minds are already clutching at countless passing phenomena, there is always the urge to gain more.

When we comprehend the entrapment and suffering brought about by our deluded involvement with the objects of our attachment—multiplied by the involvement of all other beings—we feel overwhelmed. The meaning of the phrase "ocean of samsara," so often referred to in teachings, takes on great meaning for us. We are drowning in the sufferings caused by desire.

Formal meditation gives us an arena in which to relax samsaric involvement and to recognize the actual empty nature of self and object, as well as of attachment itself. Once we are freed from delusion by the red light of

Tara, attachment in its pure energy aspect becomes the padma family's discriminating awareness, the simultaneous recognition of the empty nature and manifest details of all phenomena.

Similarly, the blue light of the vajra family purifies anger into mirror-like awareness. When adverse situations arise, the mind does not react with anger, nor does it contract into the intense object–subject duality of alienation. Rather, immovable in nondual awareness, mind simply reflects whatever arises with the brilliant clarity of a mirror.

The white light of the buddha family purifies stupidity and ignorance into the awareness of basic space. The dullness of the uncomprehending mind is thus released into the limitless recognition of nondual awareness.

The green light of the karma family purifies jealousy into all-accomplishing awareness. The keen-eyed assessments of jealousy give way to nondual recognition that accomplishment does not belong to one being or another, but exists as part of the perfection of the whole.

The yellow light of the ratna family purifies pride into the equanimity aspect of pristine awareness. Instead of elevating oneself, one recognizes the buddha nature of all beings and the empty nature of all phenomena, creating a vast expanse of equality.

The five aspects of pristine awareness have a single essence, although just as we have affinities for one color or another, we have affinities for different aspects of wisdom. Red Tara, though of the padma family, emanates all aspects of wisdom and purifies all aspects of samsaric delusion.

In formal meditation we do not focus on the conceptual meaning of this; we visualize Tara and experience her rainbow light as strongly as possible pervading all beings equally. The infinite blessing of Tara, composed of the full power of the Three Jewels and the Three Roots and the full perfection of the three kayas, is truly the illumination of pristine awareness that dissipates the force of delusion and brings recognition of mind's intrinsic buddha nature.

WHEN THE FORCE of delusion diminishes, its reflections of negative karma, sickness, demonic afflictions and obstacles also diminish. Tibetans mean various things by the word "demon," including beings in the hungry spirit realm who, because of their dissatisfaction and suffering, inflict harm on humans. We cannot see them, and they have no inherent reality, but they do have at least as much relative reality as we do in the human realm. They are constantly tormented, and we should have great compassion for them, praying that they be liberated from their suffering.

We are fascinated by demonic beings—we sometimes make horror movies out of our grotesque imaginings—but these external demons are not as relevant to our situation as internal ones: the demon of the mind's poisons, who pollutes our mindstream with hatred, doubt, fear, greed, jealousy and all the other toxins of delusion; the demon of self-pleasure, who seduces us into making ourselves comfortable instead of adhering to our altruistic intention to benefit others, who prompts us to turn on the television, CD player or VCR just when we are about to meditate, who panders to our pride by whispering, "You've done enough; you owe it to yourself"; the demon of aggregates, whose insidious self-identification causes us to contract around a fictitious self and believe the falsehood that our aggregates (form, feeling, volition, perception and consciousness) comprise an inherently existing self; and the demon of death, who plays a terrific joke on those under the sway of the demon of aggregates by stripping the self of form, feeling, volition and perception, and leaving only naked consciousness in the face of the winds of karma at the time of death.

Death likewise mocks those controlled by the demon of the mind's poisons by separating them from the objects of their projections and leaving them exposed and vulnerable to the potential for suffering that they have created. And again, death tricks those allured by the demon of pleasure by taking away the objects of their pleasure, their bodies and their senses, leaving them only a vacuum of lost opportunities.

If we do not recognize these four demons and understand how they manifest, our blind ignorance will allow them to exert their negative influence on our activities of body, speech and mind. Yet taking a hard, clear look does not mean wrestling with them. We deal with demons—with all obstacles and obscurations—by affirming our bodhichitta intention and engaging in selfless work for the welfare of all beings. We have faith and take refuge in Tara. We do the practice according to the lama's instructions, instructions that are transmitted through a perfect lineage, and we trust that the processes of the practice will liberate us from the demons of delusion.

This is not a violent purge of demons or an abrupt casting out of negativity. Rather they "evaporate like dew in the morning sun." When the short English text was compiled from the extensive Red Tara sadhana, Chagdud Rinpoche focused most specifically on this image, and in doing the practice one realizes its profound meaning beyond the mere beauty of poetic expression.

The illumination of mind brought about by Tara's wisdom blessings is the field in which all perfect qualities arise. These are Tara's qualities, and those of our own buddha nature. They include relative qualities such as wealth, well-being, beauty, longevity and spiritual connections, and the absolute qualities of pure perception and pristine awareness. They include compassion, love, joy and equanimity, generosity, moral discipline, patience, perseverance, concentration and transcendent knowledge. All without exception "increase beyond measure."

Thus, by the methods of this Red Tara meditation not only do we empty the mind of delusion, we also open the vast treasure of space where precious qualities arise spontaneously in the sphere of natural awareness.

The Jetzun Prayer:
A Word-by-Word Translation

As we recite the prayer, we envision that all beings throughout the six realms recite it with us, creating a reverberation that expands to the limits of space.

Je Tzun P'hag Ma Drol Ma Khyed Khyen No
Gal Kyen Kun Sel Sam Don Nyur Drub Dzod

Illustrious Tara, please be aware of me.
Remove my obstacles and quickly grant my
    excellent aspirations.

Je means "foremost"; *Tzun* means "venerable." *P'hag* means "exalted"; *Ma* is a feminine ending for "mother." The honorific title *Je Tzun P'hag Ma* is thus translated "illustrious."

43

Drol Ma means "mother of liberation" or "savioress," and is translated as its Sanskrit equivalent, "Tara."

Khyed is the honorific "you"; *Khyen* is "know" or, in the honorific, "be aware of"; *No* indicates an emphatic. The phrase *Khyed Khyen No* is thus translated as "please be aware of me."

Gal means "contradiction" or "counter-productive"; *Kyen* means "conditions"; *Kun* means "all"; *Sel* means "dispel" or "remove." The phrase *Gal Kyen Kun Sel* is rendered as "remove my obstacles."

Sam means "wish"; *Don* is "meaning." The phrase is rendered as "excellent aspirations." *Nyur* means "quickly"; *Drub* means "accomplish"; *Dzod* is the honorific imperative "please do it." The phrase *Sam Don Nyur Drub Dzod* is thus translated as "quickly grant my excellent aspirations."

Mantra

Tara's mantra projects the essence of her enlightened speech, described by sixty transcendent qualities, including the ability to make what is said understood simultaneously in different languages, to project the voice without strain so all can hear perfectly and to convey meaning accurately, whatever the listener's level of intelligence, as well as harmoniousness, melodiousness and clarity. Ultimately, the sound of enlightened speech—sound inseparable from emptiness—is the resonance of pristine awareness.

The mantra of Red Tara, Rigjed Lhamo, comes through the same perfect lineage transmission as the visualization. As we recite it, we establish bodhichitta intention, envisioning that all beings throughout the six realms recite with us, that they likewise benefit from the connection with Tara, specifically in the purification of speech and the increase of excellent speech qualities that are the blessings of mantra practice. The mantra is recited three, seven, twenty-one or one hundred and eight times, or in multiples of one hundred and eight, as counted on one's mala. It can be chanted according to the tune Chagdud Rinpoche teaches or recited very softly—and rapidly if one wishes—as a vibration of the voice or, more subtly, as a vibration of the breath, a resonance of mind. Whether chanted aloud or recited inaudibly, the mantra syllables should always remain distinct.

A great benefit of mantra recitation is that it constantly channels the mind's processes back into meditation. More than a simple re-minder, mantra creates a strong current of concentration that reinforces the visualiza-tion and carries one into deeper levels of real-ization. The pervasive power of sound, like that of light, dissolves the illusory separation between oneself and others. In nondual awareness, all sound is experienced as the mantra of the deity, the spontaneous reso-nance of Tara's wisdom.

Mandala Offering

Tara's generosity is unsurpassed. To bring forth our own qualities of generosity we per-form mandala offerings by offering the three-thousand-fold universe, the universe in its ex-ponential multiplicity, the limitless reaches of space and all its phenomena. In Tibetan Bud-dhist cosmology, the center of our own world system in this universe is Mount Meru, a four-sided, ziggurat-like mountain with steps and a flat top. Rising out of a scented ocean, Mount Meru is made of crystal in the east, lapis lazuli in the south, ruby in the west and gold in the north.

In the outer oceans, beyond seven mountain ranges, are the four continents, including our own southern continent of Dzambuling, each having two minor continents (subcontinents). The riches of this vast constellation are offered to Tara.

The upper elevations of Mount Meru and the uppermost plateau form the realms of worldly gods, whose resplendent displays of wealth are almost beyond human imagination. Their awesome power and glory include the power to manifest effortlessly whatever they wish in the most refined, aesthetically pleasing form. The ethereal treasures of these worldly gods are offered to Tara.

Seven concentric rings of mountains surround Meru, and in the swirling waters that separate these rings live supernatural sea creatures known as nagas. These nagas, in snakelike forms, also inhabit our own planet, and they often inflict disease and discomfort on those who pollute the environment. Although they themselves experience much suffering, they guard fantastic treasures in their realm—both sacred treasures such as texts (the Red Tara text was brought by Nagarjuna from their realm to ours) and treasures of wealth. All the treasures of the nagas are offered to Tara.

Likewise, the riches of the human realm—both the natural wonders of our earth and those wrought by human skill—are similarly offered. The offering of the "splendor and glory of gods, nagas and humans" is complete, from its inception as a positive impulse in the mind as "the roots of virtue," through its full manifestation as form, speech or thought.

In meditation we visualize this inexhaustible display as clouds of perfectly pure offerings, focusing very clearly on various aspects in beautiful detail or expansively imagining the universal offerings billowing like clouds. In visualization our mind is like a zoom lens that can instantly perceive any dimension from any vantage point. Just as the offerings are limitless, so is the mind's ability to conceive them.

The mandala offering can be recited one, three or twenty-one times; then the mantra

Tram Guru Ratna Mandala Edam Yami is recited to seal the offering. Finally, the mind is allowed to rest in natural awareness, in which ordinary delineations of oneself as the offerer, Tara as the recipient and the process of offering simply fall away.

Mandala offerings accomplish the two accumulations. The offering of substances, either actual or envisioned, accomplishes merit; the realization of the empty nature of these substances—as well as of the offerer and the recipient—accomplishes pristine awareness. As merit increases and pristine awareness unfolds, all that is tight and restrictive, bound-up self-clinging, simply dissipates. The full meaning of Tara's supreme, all-pervasive generosity reveals itself.

Prayers for Accomplishment

The next step of the practice consists of the prayers for accomplishment, which we recite while still visualizing the noble mother Tara in front of us. These prayers are requests for Tara's protection and blessings for ourselves and all beings. They are, from another point of view, the protection and blessings we ourselves hope to offer others by full realization of Tara's enlightened qualities. Certain aspects of the prayers have been explained in the previous sections or are easily understood. The following will focus on the aspects that may need some explanation.

Over time, as we continue Tara practice and pray with deep faith, different phrases in the prayers take hold in the mind and acquire rich significance. We contemplate them as we go about our daily activities, and they become sources of powerful insight. More profound realization, however, comes from meditative awareness. Just as when we allow the mind to rest in natural awareness after repetitions of prayers, mantra and mandala offerings, so we let it rest after these recitations. In this way, our prayers take the mind beyond words and concepts.

THE FIRST PRAYER, which Chagdud Rinpoche has also incorporated into the extensive Red Tara sadhana, was written by Khenpo Ngaga as part of his praises to the twenty-one Taras. An emanation of Vimalamitra, Khenpo Ngaga was an enlightened master who lived near Rinpoche's region of

Tromtar. When he wrote, "May the enlightened mind be mastered and appearances perceived purely as the deity's body," he was referring to the state of natural awareness,
completely free of delusion, in which all appearances are recognized as spontaneous expressions of Tara's form.

The phrase "may . . . harm from other beings and bad dreams be averted" might make
one wonder how dreams could cause harm.
In a certain sense, we need protection from
the negative energies presented to our consciousness in the potent symbolism of dreams.
In a different sense, we need protection from
our own tendency to be influenced by the
dream delusion. The fear generated by night-
mares, for example, can increase aversion in
daily life and, in extreme cases, can cause
physical and mental illnesses.

"May rebirth not occur in the eight states
devoid of leisure to practice" refers to the hell
realms, the hungry spirit realm, the animal
realm, the realm of long-lived gods, rebirth in
a time when there is no buddha, rebirth
among the "border tribes" in which there is
no connection to the teachings, rebirth with
mental or physical disabilities that make it

51

impossible to comprehend the teachings and rebirth among those with extremely wrong views, such as the idea that killing is virtuous or that actions have no karmic consequences.

These states are "devoid of leisure to practice" because they involve the mindstream ceaselessly in samsaric delusion. Even the realm of the gods, where there seems to be endless leisure, is actually a state of constant involvement with the false pleasures of samsara. In these eight states, there is no thought of ultimate enlightenment, no opening in the mindstream where such a thought can even occur.

"From the ripening of karma caused by delusion, grant the blessing that shields, protects and conceals" reminds us that all karma is caused by delusion. For one completely beyond delusion, remaining within the mind's natural awareness, phenomena arise and subside in and of themselves without karmic traces—as Chagdud Rinpoche sometimes says, like "writing on water."

A question often asked is why one should pray for the blessing that conceals one from one's own karma. Consider the fact that we have experienced countless cycles of existence, that we cannot remember them (most people cannot even clearly remember their childhood) and cannot know what kind of karma we have created until it ripens. When we begin spiritual practice and the purification of negative karma, we pray that past karma does not suddenly ripen and create massive obstacles that we cannot overcome at our level of practice.

For example, one of the karmic results of killing is a short life. Who of us can say that in past lives we have never been a soldier caught in the violence of war, or a hunter, or a bird of prey? If the full force of the karma of such a rebirth were to intervene, we might die before our connection to spiritual practice could become well established. Death's interruption of life would then represent a lost or greatly delayed opportunity and much more suffering. We request protection and concealment until karmic obstacles are within the reach of our ability to purify them and can become a source of realization rather than of samsaric suffering.

We should not make this request in the expectation that obstacles will never appear. The very nature of human rebirth is that of sickness, old age and death, and even great bodhisattvas are subject to these conditions. However, their experience of illness is very different from that of an ordinary person or even a less realized practitioner. For them obstacles arise and subside within the sphere of nondual awareness; their ability to purify obstacles benefits all living beings.

THE SECOND PRAYER of accomplishment comes from Apong Terton's extensive Red Tara treasure. It begins with homage to the absolute, all-encompassing Tara, who is the "spontaneous presence of the three kayas"; who "gives birth to victorious ones of the three times" (past, present, and future); who is the "sublime guide of the three realms of existence" (the formless, the form and the desire realms, the first two referring to certain worldly god realms of experience and the desire realm referring to all other realms, including the human realm); and who is "a cloud of inexhaustible bliss of the three secrets" of vajra body, vajra speech and vajra mind.

In this way we acknowledge and reverently bow before Tara as one who has attained enlightenment, who manifests infinite, all-pervasive, absolute awareness and who reveals to us our own buddha nature, no different from her own.

"From now until I reach enlightenment, I will rely on you as my sole source of refuge and protection" sometimes provokes the question, especially among those who do more than one deity practice, as to why we rely on Tara as our "sole source of refuge and protection." We need to understand that Tara, as the ultimate nature of mind, enlightened awareness, is the same as all deities. When we take refuge in her, we take refuge in all deities, in all lineage lamas and in all aspects of enlightenment. The different practices have come from the intentional mind of the Buddha to meet the different needs of sentient beings, but these practices are of one wisdom essence.

"In accordance with your former aspirations and commitments, do not waver in your compassion" refers to Tara's bodhisattva vow to save all beings from the eight great fears and to lead them to enlightenment.

"Whosoever sees me, hears me, touches me or remembers me" refers to the four means by which enlightened beings can bring about liberation. For us this may now seem overreaching, but once we attain enlightenment these become the four avenues by which the potential of our buddha nature resonates with and helps to reveal the buddha nature of sentient beings.

"Without relying on the power of magnetizing, how could one gain the necessary qualities to care for others?" asks how, if we are devoid of power to turn others' minds in a positive direction and instill in them some aspiration toward spiritual development, we can influence and care for them. The source of this charismatic power is compassion, love and the warmth of truly beneficial intention. With all the power of our heart, we wish for the well-being and ultimate enlightenment of others impartially, regardless of whether they are positive or negative, friends or enemies, virtuous or not. The goal is for samsara to be emptied of all beings "without exception."

Our connection to others develops in stages that inspire the "four kinds of devotion." First is friendship. People respond to genuine concern and goodwill from a true friend. In such a relationship, good qualities are affirmed and strengthened, and harmful habits can be corrected in a context of kindness and stability. Friendship fosters devotion based on trust.

Greater than friendship is the kindness a mother shows her child. An infant reaches to its mother not because it recognizes her face but because it senses her single-minded compassion and unconditional benevolence. A mother would give her own life for her child; the child intuits this and develops strong, loving devotion.

The relationship of sovereigns to those within their dominion is more encompassing still, for it is a sovereign's power and wisdom that provide well-being and protection from harm to those within his or her sphere of authority. Devotion to a sovereign is imbued with respect and a willingness to serve a higher goal.

Unsurpassed is the relationship between lama and students. The lama embodies the Buddha's intention to lead all beings to a state of enlightenment, to his wisdom and his compassion. Because it is not now possible to receive teachings directly from the Buddha, the lama shows students greater, more direct kindness than the Buddha himself. The lama's realization forms a mold for students, and finally, when spiritual training is completely accomplished, there is no difference between the lama's mind and the students'. As students experience the inner changes brought about by the lama's guidance, devotion evolves from simple faith to overwhelming respect and reverence.

Once these relationships are established, how does one actually "influence all those to be tamed"? Someone asked Chagdud Rinpoche whether a bodhisattva should give others what they want or what they need. "Want" was defined as the changeable desires of samsara and "need" as the underlying necessity to find the dharma and attain buddhahood. Rinpoche answered that a bodhisattva should always fulfill spiritual needs to the extent possible but not lose connection with people by ignoring their ordinary wishes.

Even bodhisattvas beleaguered by the poisonous minds of very nonvirtuous people are often able, by working with great skill on many different levels, to tame their minds and meet their true needs without breaking their connection with them. Yeshe Tsogyal, the wisdom consort of Guru Rinpoche and an emanation of Tara, was once offered a poisoned drink by a jealous queen. Though she knew it was poisoned, Yeshe Tsogyal took the drink anyway, then sang this verse:

> Listen dear friend, this nectar is wonderful,
>   the very essence of goodness;
> My body is the Vajra Body, unsullied and
>   indestructible.
> It has transmuted this nectar into the
>   wondrous essence of immortality.
> Though this purpose of yours has not been
>   fulfilled,
> I have turned it to great fulfillment.

When she finished singing, she became radiant with rainbows and lights that shimmered to the very tips of her hair.

"Upon mastering positive qualities within a state of liberation" refers to the fact that one can be liberated into a pure realm beyond suffering without being fully enlightened. In such a realm one listens to teachings and meditates until ultimate truth awakens the mind to a state of pristine awareness. At that instant, one attains the "actual form of the victorious ones, resplendent with the major and minor marks of perfection"—marks that include images of wheels on the palms and soles, a perfectly proportioned body, light shining from the forehead and slightly webbed fingers and toes.

"May the yogas of the two stages be mastered" refers to the development and completion stages of practice. The development stage encompasses all the processes of visualization and recitation, and the completion stage includes resting nondually in one's own natural awareness.

Transformation into the Wisdom Body of Tara

Visualization

Initiation into the Apong Terton lineage of Red Tara empowers practitioners to follow the prayers for accomplishment with the development stage of visualizing themselves as Red Tara. Empowerment is necessary for this stage, self-visualization, because it increases the mind's receptivity to the blessings of the lineage lamas and opens the possibility of full realization. While by visualizing and praying to the deity's outer form we remove obstacles and establish good conditions, it is empowerment that enables us to actualize Tara's qualities of enlightened body, speech and mind.

We first relax the mind, allowing ordinary appearances and the habit of holding to them as solid to subside, to recede from our consciousness, so that we experience the nature of nondual emptiness. This emptiness is not nothingness, for it is the source of all phenomena. The experience of pure phenomena begins with clarity, a spontaneous focusing of the mind's natural energy that gives rise to the pure appearance of the seed syllable *Tam*. It is a seed syllable in the sense that from it evolves the entire display of Red Tara, her retinue and her pure realm. Thus, *Tam* transforms into the luminous form of Tara—meaning that one's own body transforms into the wisdom body of Tara—with the Buddha Amitabha above the head, in her pure realm of Yulokod, the Land of Turquoise Leaves.

The fullness of this inner aspect of Tara practice corresponds in large degree to the depth of our realization of emptiness. Although we must exert ourselves conceptually in creating and sustaining the visualization, we also develop a sense of great spaciousness, a recognition that this is the spontaneous display of pure phenomena. Tara's form is not some imaginative artwork; it is the effortless expression of the qualities of enlightenment. One might say that Tara's ruby-red color symbolizes discriminating awareness, love and the lotus family. From a more profound perspective, one would say that from the emptiness of dharmakaya, replete with the full potential of phenomena, the color red manifests as the pure display of discriminating awareness, of love and of the lotus family. What this means in meditation is that the deeper we relax into intrinsic awareness, buddha nature, emptiness, the more natural and genuine the qualities of visualization become. Nothing need be fabricated; we recognize our buddha nature as the ground from which arises the pure appearance of Tara.

The visualization is set forth in traditional sequence, but the focus during any particular meditation session may vary. For example, as Tara's blessings radiate to the beings of the six realms, often specific conditions of suffering arise in one's consciousness—the problems of a friend perhaps, a natural disaster or some catastrophic war. It is not incorrect to focus compassion on such situations in that moment, but we should always maintain a profound impartiality. All beings suffer, not just our acquaintances or those we see or hear about, but also those in realms unseen. Likewise, from now until they reach enlightenment, all beings benefit from Tara's blessings.

After the visualization is established, the

repetition of mantra begins. Tara's mantra is repeated seven, twenty-one or one hundred and eight times or in multiples of one hundred and eight, as counted on a mala. In her heart, the mantra syllables are arranged around the perimeter of a sun disk cupped in a red lotus, the letters facing inward around the seed syllable *Tam*. As one repeats *Om Tare Tam Soha*, the mantra mala revolves in a counterclockwise direction, sending forth light in all directions.

As with every vajrayana practice, the benefits are both for oneself and for others. Thus, Tara's radiance first invokes the blessings of the wisdom deities, benefiting oneself. Then it extends to the beings of the six realms, benefiting others. Sometimes practitioners have difficulty experiencing the radiance and reconvergence of light, but if they relax deeply into the true nature of mind and focus lightly on the visualization, it becomes very natural. In that context, all phenomena are perceived in their inherent purity, their empty essence. All are transformed by awareness into the display of Tara's pure realm.

Completion Stage

At the end of mantra recitation, Tara's form dissolves into emptiness. We recite the syllable *Ah*, the essence of emptiness, three times. Then we rest in effortless, nondual awareness until thoughts intervene. The next moment represents one of the pivotal points of practice: arising concepts mark the closure of the nondual, nonconceptual completion stage, but it is the opening of another phase of meditation in which all forms are experienced as the body of the deity, all sounds as the speech of the deity and all thoughts as the mind of the deity. This recognition of the pure nature of all phenomena beyond any stain of attachment or aversion, awareness beyond any trace of delusion, is the key point of vajrayana deity practice.

By holding pure perception of form, sound and thought as the display of the enlightened body, speech and mind of Red Tara, we integrate practice into daily life. Chagdud Rinpoche emphasizes this aspect, because formal sitting practice is not enough. If one climbs a mountain one hour a day and rests on a plateau for the other twenty-three, the ascent will be very slow. Ideally, meditation should be sustained not only in sitting and daily-life practice throughout the day, but also at night, when Tara dream yoga can be practiced by those who have received instructions.

If one falters in such extensive meditation, at least one should turn one's mind toward practice as often as possible throughout the day. Rinpoche has said that even a passing insect may receive benefit from one's murmured mantra or compassionate wish. He encourages everyone to lose no opportunity to create virtue through offering, purification and dedication. In the words of Shakyamuni Buddha, "Tame your own mind. Do no harm whatsoever. Practice virtue thoroughly."

Closing Prayers

Dedication

All Tibetan Buddhist sadhanas close with prayers of dedication. The merit of one's practice is dedicated to the welfare of sentient beings, so that temporarily their happiness increases and ultimately they find liberation.

So few beings have the opportunity to generate merit; most—particularly those myriad beings in the three lower realms—are completely enveloped in karmic patterns that create harm for others and more suffering for themselves. Practitioners are among the fortunate few, and nothing is lost by completely, openhandedly dedicating the merit of one's practice to others. Like a raindrop dissolving into the ocean, one's merit becomes part of the limitless benefit the buddhas and bodhisattvas emanate for sentient beings.

Dedicating the merit protects practitioners from developing false pride in practice and from undercutting, by nonvirtue, the merit they have generated. The merit is dedicated; there is no clinging; one generates more. Even in the moment of the dedication of merit as one rests in a state of emptiness, realization increases.

Prayer of Aspiration

On the threshold of becoming enlightened buddhas, bodhisattvas offer a prayer establishing their individual aspiration. Tara's prayer of aspiration as a bodhisattva was to bring swift blessings and to liberate from the eight great fears anyone who calls her name. In this aeon there will be 1,002 buddhas, of which Shakyamuni was the fourth. The Tara sadhana incorporates the aspiration prayer of Moypa, the last and smallest of future buddhas, whose aspiration will encompass the prayers of all buddhas who precede him.

The Auspicious Wish

The auspicious wish, written by His Holiness Dudjom Jigdral Yeshe Dorje, head of the

Nyingmapa lineage until his death in 1987, rings out with clarity. It is what all people of goodwill wish for all humankind.

Long-Life Prayer for Chagdud Tulku Rinpoche

At the request of Chagdud Rinpoche's students, His Holiness Khyentse Rinpoche composed this prayer for Rinpoche's longevity. The first line invokes Guru Rinpoche—Padmasambhava—who "attained the kaya of deathlessness." When Padmasambhava left our world for the subcontinent of Ngayab, he did not have to undergo the transition of ordinary death. Instead, his corporeal form became a rainbow body and he disappeared into the sky. Completely victorious over the limits imposed by death, he still appears to certain fortunate practitioners in his luminous rainbow form.

As already discussed, the "Three Roots" refers to the lama, yidam and dakini, and "lord of the dance" is a translation of one of Chagdud Rinpoche's dharma names, Gargyi Wangkhyug. The "three secrets," as mentioned earlier in the explanation of the prayer for accomplishment, are the secrets of vajra body, speech and mind, which are self-secret to those who have not realized their essence as emptiness, as awareness.

Feast Offering and
Meditation for the Dead

The Tsok Offering

The eighth and twenty-third days of each lunar month are especially auspicious times to perform a feast offering (Tib. *tsok*) in conjunction with Red Tara practice. "Tsok" means "gathering," the gathering together of practitioners who maintain samaya, the gathering by invitation of the mandala of deities and the gathering of various offering substances—food, drink, lights, incense and flowers—that embody skillful means and transcendent knowledge.

Tsok is the most excellent method of making offerings. Meat and alcohol are essential, and these along with the other offering substances constitute the material aspect of the tsok. The imagined aspect involves reciting *Ram Yam Kham* while visualizing wisdom fire incinerating the material offering substances, wisdom wind scattering them and wisdom water cleansing them so that impure perceptions and grasping at the seeming reality and ordinary characteristics of these substances are purified into emptiness.

The levels of tsok offerings are referred to in the line "The outer, inner and secret offerings amass like glorious clouds." We recite the syllables *Om Ah Hung Ho*. From emptiness, from the syllable *Ah*, appears a skullcup equal in size to the three-thousand-fold universe within which the offering substances exist as the nature of pristine awareness. From their vapors arise clouds of offerings that fill all of space. This is the outer tsok feast of an inexhaustible array of the five sensory pleasures. With the recitation of *Om*, the substances are transformed into the nature of the five meats and five nectars. With *Hung*, the substances are transformed and consecrated as the nature of inexhaustible nectar of pristine awareness, expanding to fill the limits of space with clouds of offerings. With *Ho*, the offerings are imbued with power to delight the deities. This whole process pertains to the outer tsok offering.

The inner tsok offering is made within the vessel of the subtle body's three channels and five chakras, with the *tummo* fire (the mystic fire of inner heat) blazing upward and releasing a flow of pure nectar from a white *Hang* syllable in the crown of the head. This blending of white and red energies into the nectar of bodhichitta, the union of bliss and emptiness, pervades all the subtle channels and chakras.

The secret tsok offering takes place within what is termed the "vessel of the ultimate ground of all experience," atemporal and pristine. The tsok offering arranged therein is that of self-occurring intrinsic awareness. The dynamic energy and radiance of intrinsic awareness manifest as adornments, that is, as spontaneously present appearances of phenomena.

The second line ("Arya Tara . . .") constitutes the invitation of the guests who are to be the recipients of the tsok offering, and the offering itself. The noble Red Tara, in whom the Three Jewels unite, and her retinue of the entire assembly of the Three Roots are invited to the space in front of oneself and requested to remain in order to receive the offerings. The sacred bond with the deities is fulfilled by their delight in the consecrated offerings. The two accumulations of merit and pristine awareness are perfected, and prayers are made for the bestowal of the sublime siddhi, or spiritual attainment, of enlightenment and more common siddhis, such as flying, passing through solid substances and clairvoyance.

Following this first stage of the tsok offering, the second stage ("Before you . . .") again delights the deities. The second offering is a means of confessing and atoning for the effects of harmful actions—the ten nonvirtues in general and especially infractions of the vows of individual ordination, bodhisattva vows or samaya commitments of the holders of intrinsic awareness (Tib. *rig dzin*).

In the third stage of the offering ("By liberation . . ."), all the obstacles that interfere with our path to liberation and our ultimate attainment of omniscience—all the "rudras" of grasping at self and object—are conceived of as nondual. The offering is visualized as enemies and hindrances that are summoned, held, bound and rendered insensible by the force of the four immeasurable qualities of equanimity, compassion, love and joy. Finally, the visualized forms of obstruction are liberated by the weapon of realization of non-self. The resulting heaps of flesh, blood and bones embody the poisonous emotions of ignorance, attachment and anger, which are offered to all the deities of the Three Roots. Through this offering ("Through pristine awareness . . .") of liberation of the rudras of grasping at self and object, the mind-stream is blessed with the unsurpassable siddhi—the wisdom of the three secrets of enlightened form, speech and mind.

As for the guests who partake of the remainders ("May you guests . . ."), although the essential nature of the deities is of a single mandala with no hierarchy, for the purpose of taming beings manifestations of principal deities, their closely connected retinues and more distant retinues appear. Thus, remainders are collected and offered to those who dwell in the outer circles of the mandala and who are enjoined to carry out the four activities of pacification, enrichment, power and wrath: pacification of illnesses, demonic influences and the effects of harmful actions and obscurations; enrichment by increasing merit, wisdom, wealth, excellent qualities and longevity; power by bringing confused appearances under control within the expanse of intrinsic awareness; wrath by liberating outer, inner and secret obstacles in unborn basic space.

The remainders are offered with the prayer that the entire array of enlightened activities be accomplished so that individuals fully realize dharmakaya for their own benefit and simultaneously manifest the form kayas (Skt. *rupakaya*) for the benefit of others.

The ritual of offering is carried out by placing the first three portions of tsok on the shrine as an offering to Tara and her retinue, offering the fourth portion to the lama and sharing the rest equally among the participants. Each person should receive at least a small piece of meat and a spoonful of alcohol with the other tsok substances. While partaking of the tsok feast, we should not think of the offerings as ordinary food and drink that we either like or dislike. Rather, we should partake of the tsok with devotion and appreciation for the liberation that takes place by simply tasting it. The inherent nature of the body is that of aggregates and elements of masculine and feminine buddhas of the five families. Our sense faculties and their objects are of the nature of the masculine and feminine bodhisattvas; our limbs, the nature of the masculine and feminine wrathful deities. This is termed the "body mandala of the three planes," and when we partake of the tsok, it is as the inexhaustible nectar of pristine awareness that delights the deities of this mandala.

By its very nature, tsok creates a sixfold satisfaction: the deities are satisfied by the offerings; the practitioners are satisfied by the food and drink; the wisdom mandala is satisfied by the subtle essence of nectar; the deities of one's body are satisfied by the pristine awareness of bliss and emptiness; dakinis on the outer and inner levels are satisfied by the offering of song and dance; the dharma protectors who carry out activity are satisfied by the offering of remainders.

The tsok is offered within the context of the three concepts: the lama is understood to be the heruka, that is, the embodiment of all phenomena, inseparable from emptiness; one's fellow participants are understood to be masculine and feminine deities; the tsok substances are understood to be the substances that confer siddhis.

The tsok is performed after the mantra section of "Transformation into the Wisdom Body of Tara" but before the dissolution. Recitation of the two-line Jetzun Prayer takes place as the tsok is passed around, and other prayers of aspiration—including the Orgyan Prayer at the end of the practice text—and those for the longevity of the lamas may be included.

Tara Meditation for the Dead

This section of the sadhana was written by Chagdud Rinpoche to provide a means by which Tara practitioners can benefit the deceased. Those who have accomplished Tara practice thoroughly, even in this very concise format, have established the potential to gain their own liberation by recognizing the display that arises during death's transition as inseparable from Tara's enlightened form, speech and mind. Or if one simply maintains devotion and the habit of prayer as one traverses the intermediate state between death and rebirth (Tib. *bar do*), then merely invoking Tara's blessing by calling her name will release one from turmoil and uncertainty either into Tara's pure realm or into a high rebirth conducive to the continuation of one's dharma path.

Tara meditation or the accomplishment of other relatively easy methods such as transference of consciousness at the moment of death (Tib. *p'ho wa*) should instill confidence in practitioners about their own death process, but the methods for liberating deceased friends, family members and acquaintances are generally quite complicated and require a vajra master skilled in ritual. Nonetheless, to benefit the deceased, we may use this short, powerful, direct meditation, which relies on the interdependence of Tara's enlightened intention to rescue beings, the blessings of the lama, the practitioner's love and compassion and dedication of merit to the deceased.

Visualizing either Tara in the space in front of us, or ourselves transformed into the wisdom body of Tara, we meditate that rainbow light shines from Tara's heart throughout the six realms and the bardo and envelops the deceased wherever they are, "purifying their karma and infusing them with Tara's ra-

diant blessing." The more profound our realization of emptiness, the deeper is our experience that this is actually the case—not merely
imagined light washing over imagined figures
of the deceased, but mind's unobstructed
quality of sheer clarity encompassing the
mindstreams of the deceased, purifying and
blessing them, bringing forth their natural radiance, which dissolves into Tara's enlightened expanse.

The practice is done for forty-nine days
after death, usually the longest time one is in
the bardo before rebirth. After each session,
we dedicate the merit of the practice, for
whether the deceased is still in the bardo or
has been reborn, the dedication will be of
benefit.

Tara as a Daily Practice

THIS CHAPTER BRIEFLY outlines how a Tara practitioner might structure his or her daily meditation. Upon awakening, one rejoices in the advent of another day. Many people die unexpectedly in the night, but now there is at least one more day, filled with limitless spiritual opportunities. One then reflects on samsaric conditions and generates compassion and love for all beings, holding them all equal to one's own mother in loving kindness, rejoicing in any virtue they have created and in the happiness it brings them.

Knowing that without the support of practice, one has little power in the face of samsaric delusion, one then takes refuge in Tara and prays that her blessings will flow as a pervasive current during this day and that benefit will be created through every activity of body, speech and mind. The vows of refuge and bodhichitta may be stated in the words of the Tara text or in one's own words, but it is useful to allow time to contemplate and pray in this way rather than to jump out of bed and rush heedlessly into ordinary activity.

Sunrise and sunset, when the sky is red, are particularly powerful times to perform Red Tara practice. One may wish to do one's first formal meditation session early in the morning. For many Tara practitioners, a personal shrine becomes a focal point of meditation. This is not difficult to create. A traditional shrine would include an image of the deity (a photograph, statue or painting), seven water offering bowls set out in a straight line and an arrangement of special offerings of incense, flowers, food, tea and candles or butterlamps. Other items such as photographs of one's lamas and dharma gifts one has received could also find a place on the shrine. Texts should occupy a shelf above the shrine if possible, or at least in a high place and never on the floor.

In the morning one opens the shrine by filling the water bowls left to right, lighting incense and a candle, as well as offering tea (or alcohol) and food in a small glass and dish. (It is best to make fresh tea and to keep a special bag of cookies or other food used only for this purpose.) One recites *Om Ah Hung* as these offerings of substance are multiplied without limit through mantra and visualization. The water is visualized as billowing clouds of pure offerings and qualities that are presented to all the buddhas and bodhisattvas, particularly to Red Tara and her retinue of twenty Taras. They receive these offerings with great rejoicing, and their blessings shower on the practitioner and all sentient beings.

Similarly, incense is imagined to pervade the universe with a delightful scent that purifies sickness and obscuration and expresses the perfect discipline of the dharma. Light becomes complete illumination, and when one offers flowers, they fill all of samsara and nirvana with loveliness and with pleasure in their beauty. Food and drink are transformed into nectar, absolutely satisfying.

During the day one adds to the offering a bit of one's own food and drink as nectar to all wisdom beings before one partakes of them, then imagines that they are returned as wisdom blessings and nourishment to all.

There are many profound teachings on the nature of offerings, especially as related to Tara practice. However, the essential point is to make offerings with the supreme generosity characteristic of Tara. Such generosity creates a foundation of nonattachment and open awareness that increases the accumulations of both merit and pristine awareness.

At night one empties the water bowls, right to left, dries them and turns them upside down. At bedtime one reflects on the day, honestly assessing one's conduct of body, speech and mind. Visualizing Tara in front, one expresses remorse for any downfalls, vows not to repeat them and then receives the radiance of Tara's blessing. Whatever virtue one has created is dedicated to the welfare of all beings with the wish that all will find enlightenment equal to Tara's own.

Then one reflects on impermanence and prays that if death should occur in the night, Tara will be one's guide in the bardo so that the path to liberation will not be lost either in that transition or in future lifetimes. The two-line Jetzun Prayer is then recited at least seven times.

If one has had Tara dream yoga instructions, dream meditation should be undertaken just before sleep.

These daily practices—outlined here very briefly and simply—have a profound effect because they are the means by which the practitioner continually invokes Tara's blessings. Like the sun's display of rainbow light in a crystal, Tara's blessings activate the radiant reality of one's innate buddha nature.

May it be so for all beings.